David And Goliath

Storyline **Pamela Consuegra**
Illustrations **Steven Butler**

David took care of his family's sheep. He would lead the sheep to streams of water where they could drink. He would lead the sheep to green fields where they could eat grass.

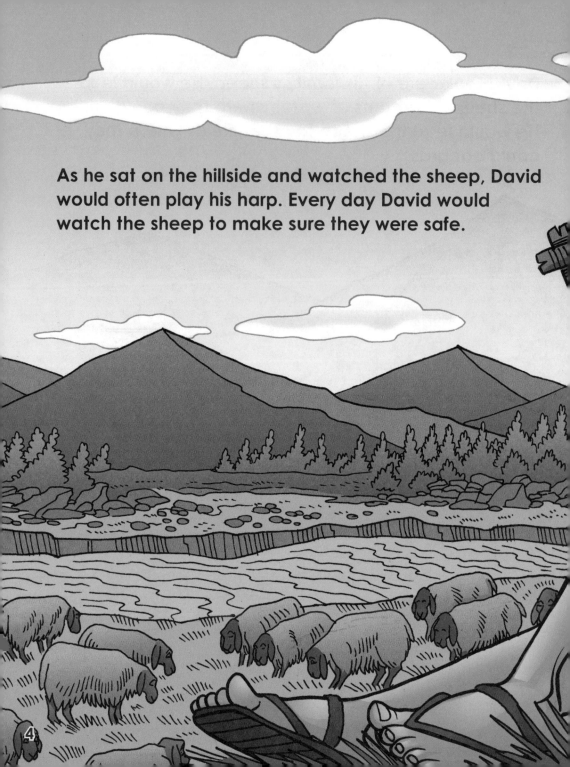

As he sat on the hillside and watched the sheep, David would often play his harp. Every day David would watch the sheep to make sure they were safe.

4

Once David used his sling to kill a lion that attacked the sheep. Another time David killed an angry bear. God watched over David every day and helped him.

One day David's father said, "David, I want you to take some food to your brothers who have gone to war. It will be a long walk, but I trust you to do this job well."

David said, "I will go. I know God will be with me. God protected me from the bear and the lion. I know he will watch over me."

David began walking to the place where his brothers were camped. He walked for a long time. Soon he could see the tents of the army in the distance.

When he reached the tents, David quickly spotted his brothers. He ran to meet them. He had missed them very much, and was happy to see them again.

Suddenly David heard a booming voice. "Send out a man to fight me!" David looked across the valley and there stood the biggest man he had ever seen.

"Who is that?" asked David.

"That is Goliath," his brothers said. "He is the champion of the Philistine army. He is a giant! Every day he challenges our army, but no one wants to fight him."

"I will go and fight this man," said David. "I know that God will help me. God helped me kill a bear and a lion. I am sure he will help me now."

So David's brothers took him to their leader, King Saul.

"King Saul," said David, "Let me go and fight this giant. "I know that God will help me."

King Saul looked at David. "This young man is the only one willing to fight," said the King. He turned to David. "Here is my armor. You may wear it to protect you."

David put the King's armor on his legs. He put it on his arms. He put it on his chest. He put the King's heavy helmet on his head.

But the armor was too big and too heavy for David. He could not even walk! "I do not need this armor," said David. "God will protect me."

So David took off the King's armor. He picked up his sling and began walking towards the Philistine camp. He walked toward the hill where Goliath was shouting, "Send out a man to fight me!"

Goliath looked at David, then he looked again. He stopped shouting. Was this a trick? Was this a joke? Was he seeing things?

Goliath pushed back his helmet to get a better look. Then he started laughing. "What is this? Am I a little dog that you have sent a boy to fight me?"

Goliath laughed and laughed.

But David ignored Goliath's laughter. "I know God will help me," he said to himself. "I know I can do amazing things because God gives me strength."

David crossed the creek bed at the bottom of the valley. He bent down and picked up five smooth stones.

David placed one of the stones in his sling, then he ran toward Goliath. David knew that God was with him.

"I come to you in the name of the Lord," David shouted. "And God will deliver you into my hand!"

As Goliath began to walk toward him, David spun his sling around and around. Suddenly he let go, and the little stone flew straight towards Goliath!

Smack! The little stone hit Goliath right in the middle of his forehead. The giant stumbled and fell down. As the Philistines stood amazed, the army of Israel rushed to attack.

"Thank you, Lord!" said David. "Thank you for watching over me, and helping us defeat your enemies."